The Gun Charge

Samuel Austin

Agent name: Samuel Austin

THE GUN CHARGE

BY

Samuel Austin

Approximately 90,000 words

Special note about me and inspirations

Samuel Austin loving caring father of two young boys loving and happy husband to a great woman. To her I must say thank you for the love you given the support that you give the care you put into not only me but our kids even though one you did not birth you cultivated a bond and relationship with my first born that healed me in so many ways I can even speak.

As a black man who been beaten broken and spit back out to know that each day you look at me as if I am the most specialist person you ever met. Fills my heart my mind with the fuel and courage to face anything. You have transformed me into the man I am today you seen the version of me that I wanted to be not the one everyone else wanted to make me. You love me for me flaws in all that's so rare. Why I can't give up all we need is one person to believe in us the way you and I believe in each other.

    This story I'm sharing is just another testimony of life and its many struggles that millions of people face every day but may not be handle or even told the way I'm telling it and sharing it. My wife idea was not to let the pain, and the situation control me but control it, use it as you have sons and friends who look to you as a mentor and a guiding light in this world. Nothing is black and white, there are so many shades and colors in between that. I have become one of the candles, voices for the unheard and forgotten the ones no one cares about the ones who don't fit in. I am just speaking my truths I hope you all enjoy!

The table of contents is just a brief timeline, as the real-life story may go back in forth with events. To help explain events and feelings that occurred during the overall story that takes place in the Samuel story the Gun charge.

Table of Contents

[Chapter 1] The Weekend Getaway 1

The day of

Arrest...

....3

[Chapter 2] Arrested.............................. 14

3 Day in cells 14

The trauma begins

[Chapter 3] the trial and journey 35

Extra: Collections of poems written randomly by Author during journey of writing the book.

[CHAPTER 1] — THE WEEKEND GETWAY

[Opening Mini vacation]

It starts on a wonderful day. Just came back from a little weekend getaway with the family. Iggy, our son, was invited to a pool party for his best friend Lia. This is a 4-year-olds party so of course parents must attend. So why not treat my wife to a weekend getaway? Plus, it is close to the house. I can make evening plans with the fellas, while she hangs with her lady friends. "Ring" pops in law calls. What are my plans for the weekend? Me Nothing but this kids party. Pops in law Trying to hit the range Saturday? Me Surely. So now I have something for me to do besides hold Iggy in the pool as he pretends to swim. Mr. love water will not touch it if I am not there.

Enjoy my time with kids in the pool, post pics of hotel room and me and my boys in the pool and jacuzzi shoot out to the Marriott Newport Nj love them for local stays. Right next to Newport mall. Lol that is my fake attempt at social media via book marketing today. Joking just placing locations to paint a picture of location. We live in Bayonne NJ, so we traveled via our car to the hotel and parking was free. Back to the story. Friday to Sunday was our booking Saturday the Lia party. Aisha my wife clocks out of work 4:30 pm Est Friday we leave check in by like 5:45 pm I state we will do dinner tonight going out tomorrow she says okay.

  My plans were canceled by 7:30 pm. Now I realize I need to secure a firearm for the weekend as it is no need to go back home, and I am still out with my family. So, I got my car when my firearm was always secured in its travel case. My firearm is legal. Due to the weight of the luggage and other equipment in trunk. The travel case clasp shifted broke. The lock keeps it from opening, but it is no longer secured for me.

So now I put it in a laptop bag that was just in my trunk for travel purposes the kids iPads games and my laptop usually go in this bag now. As my wife and I both work remotely, it's going on for 6 years at this point. With the firearm locked in bag and locked in a case I secured in safety inside my hotel room. Now that plans been canceled, I clear my mind with some Mary Jane.

Now that I am cool, I commit to family weekend just us plan out dinner and just fun things to do. We swim, we play, we eat, we explore, the more we do a little shopping. Sunday, we checked out my wife wants to stop at a few stores in Secaucus. Thrift shop etc. which is still early, and it is Sunday. We already planned out dinner by getting an affordable pizza from Sam's club.

We ended up getting home late. So, I am dropping my oldest home Josh like 9:30 pm eastern. Got home to work to try to work on this beat I purchased from one of my closet producer friends. I could not lock it in, plus I got to work in the morning.

I have been working at a new job for the past three, going on in the fourth week. I work 4 days a week for 4 hrs. a day part time in NYC. So as normally I do not accept office positions, I made an exception. Short project and good pay thirty-two. Hourly so I could pass it up. Regret that decision. Prior to my last day, Thursday, I was in a situation that was made public but not a serious situation. Where a rule instated by the company for temporary employees to follow. Me and a coworker were allowed to break the rule. Which was then bought up by a coworker.

We ended up discussing it on Friday over the phone, me, and my coworker. Squashing a sense of relief came over me. Now to break down what happened. An" IT admin" was our title at CPG church pension group. My responsibility was repairing and diagnosing the inventory equipment laptops mobile device iPad iPhone and other supported devices android Aswell other electronic carriers. Due to them having a lot of devices a lot of security protocols are set in place to prevent stealing. One of which is the iPads that are locked via a security badge which gives access to room to get into. Also, the room has it is on a private network needed to configure all devices for the organization.

Yet for the most part you sit at a desk in a cubicle because they do not trust anyone in the room. It also acts as the service desk manager's office. Now they have another rule that prevents temporary employees (temps) from getting access. So, the only way for me and my coworker to get in is if a designated employee lets us in. So, we would each grab ten devices at a time, no more than thirty. It was a step-by-step process which we had to follow so it was much configuration going on for the first two and half weeks.

More of gather information on each device and see the state inside of their ticketing software. 3 weeks in employee were just giving us their badge and asking us tomorrow to give it back once done.

Management idea. When I overheard an employee ha ha heeing. With someone who looks like an executive or management.

Saying that oh if I were to use someone else badge that would be a step into my office and then made a reference to a newly safeguarding the company video that was mandatory for everyone to watch that week. So, I said something to manager and to coworker to be safe you know Cya cover your ass. Then spoke about it to the employee directly.

It is hard world, so I felt as Black men. It is already an uncomfortable workplace for us most places we go. The field we are in is so few of us. Not asking you not to compete but let us not make our experience dreadful. We ended our conversation by saying we would go for lunch next time we work together.

Not going to be specific as to the exact day and month. Summertime July though. I know you are wondering why he went from the weekend before the work week. Answers will be revealed as I continue to share my story. As we start Monday next week where our story truly begins. Can you imagine rushing to be on time to work at 8:45 am and you drop your kid at daycare at 8 am. Leaving you forty minutes to make it to work on time!

While traveling between states and parking your vehicle you must take public transportation as the vehicle is shared between you and your spouse. These are just one of the many reasons why a mistake occurred on my end.

[The Day of Arrest]

Which leads us to the start of my workday and the story I wish to share with the world. My experiences which so many over the globe are facing and suffering. Which I will share more of my opinion as man who has overcome the oppression that is felt in Black America. So, my wife and I start by prepping the kids for their day at school or day care. Followed by securing parking to prevent street sweepers from ticketing the car as they do street cleaning. So off I go to drop My youngest to daycare to come back home park the car and make my way to New York Via public transportation. Not packing my own equipment for work due to late night from vacation prior and almost over sleeping. My normal book bag is disposed I grab the back with the lightest stuff which is also a laptop bag.

Which at the time was being used to facilitate the firearm from my car back to the house. Now my office is locked by a Key and my closet has a locked install with padlock. Inside of my closet is a safe where I secured my firearm normally.

Due to arriving late I locked the firearm and bag in the closet. I rushed to take my youngest to the bathroom and next thing you know I forgot to put firearm in bag being so tired from trip. Pass out wake up and back to where we were at before I drifted off.

Grabbing my equipment for work so I now unlock my closet door, grab the laptop bag and start packing it. Laptop in, wire bag (headset traveling bag substitute) which I have 5 of them from over the years. The bag itself is convenient for my field of work. I use one for my headset, a bag for wires and charges mouse, etc. and a bag for USB flash drives and whatever else I don't want in my pockets.

The first mistake I make is not checking to ensure that my firearm is locked safely. The second mistake I made was not double checking as normally I have all I need for work before leaving the house. Oh well! I proceed as if I have all I need because it's me, I'm always on top of things. Third mistake getting too cocky as I am doing well in life everything is going amazing in my life. So off I go to work ignoring spider senses to say.

Where just because of the color of my skin I move so cautiously in life. Just to avoid any situation like what I am facing today. I'm also late but it's a lite weak manager is out and almost finish with the task for the week on my end. I could have taken the day off.

Yet it's only three to four hours, why not bang that out right quickly. I get to the office and start taking my stuff out for work. My coworker requested that I borrow a USB that I normally supply for Apple MacBook provisioning upgrading the operation systems of the company devices from Mojave to Monterey and or Big sur at the time. Windows 8 to windows 10 or windows 11 if device would allow it.

    The same coworker is the coworker I started with. A young man won't name him but he 22 fresh out of college being 35 and living in the same state we share some interest and like minds. Being the man I am I try to pass along any positive information I can to anyone trying to do positive things. So not only have I treated this young man to lunch because we just starting and traveling is expensive. I passed knowledge and gladly shared my equipment that I paid for and took the time to set up just for the task made at least six USB bootable images to use. It took about sixteen hours in total.

Which is something he could have done himself. My experience years in Information technology is why pay rates were drastically different. However, due to the color of my skin and my coworker felt he should have gotten the same pay rate as me. Even though it's my first job and fresh out of college. So up till this day he has been acting a little funny towards me.

I ignored another mistake, so on this day we were both late and I answered his question by letting him know I had forgotten it and brought the wrong bag. This is when I realize what bag I brought and then I start to panic. I go outside to make a call to my wife and let her know the mistake I made, and I am on my way home. I go back upstairs and begin to prepare to leave. I got interrupted by another coworker who was at lunch who had a minor misunderstanding. We resolved the prior weekend before we went to enjoy our weekends.

The misunderstanding involved a joke made about a security policy that was not being followed by either me or the coworker I started with. The policy was not being followed due to orders given by the manager. The joke he made was about a training video about bade policy usage. Such as never letting another person use your badge to get into any door even if they sit right next to you or are your manager. However, since my coworker and I were only contract workers our badges did not have clearance to get into certain areas.

    The manager felt due to the contract period only being eight weeks it was not necessary for us to get clearance. Now the joke he the coworker made was not on me but including me using me as an example of the unfair treatment being displayed by the company as manager forcing people to break policy and if something were to go wrong the first ones, they would hold accountable is all of those they told to break the procedures.

    Me and my coworker who had the misunderstanding both share the same race. So not only did we understand each other we became closer. Me being new employee who is black in the industry where its already racially segregated. The last thing either one of us wants is to mess up any opportunity for a black man. So, we wanted to grab lunch publicly to ensure the company eyes knew there were no hard feelings. Due to me being late he went to lunch but had a few minutes left on his lunch as I had 10 mins left on my 15-minute break.

He asks me to go out for a smoke with him, sure no problem. We leave, walk around the corner, we speak for a while I tell him I have got to leave as I'm not trying to waste that much time but get home. I headed towards the office. Boom! Cops hop out draw guns at me. I am arrested outside right in front of my job.

[CHAPTER 2] ARRESTED

3 DAY IN CELLS

The story starts here. The officers start to handcuff me I ask what I am being arrested for. Officer says the is a crime reported in progress, which I match the description. They search for my persons to find nothing on me. I am puzzled because I know I am black but how many black men with dreads are wearing red Chinos black and red Prada's shoes and black and white stripped button-down shirt. Me being an analyzer professionally start breaking down the situation. It's not weed, nor have I stolen anything or threatened anyone so before they even put me in the car, I put two and two together. Somone went through my bag while I was gone and discovered a firearm, which right away informed the officer I mistakenly brought my legal firearm on me.

Officers inform me I am now being detained for possession of a firearm. I am driven 15 minutes away from work and still in Manhattan, a very nice area. At least until you enter the police station, that is. Through the detainee entrance it's one of the most disgusting sights you will see. Instantly smell sewer and shit odor lingers everywhere. Rats show you to your cell right along with the officers. More their home than yours and they let you know that. So, now no sleeping for me. The very first words I hear from another detained person are screams. Ouch oh shit the rats biting me. I am placed in a cell by myself for the most part everyone was.

In the cells next to me was a young man who was arrested for grand larceny out of Macy's and had almost 10,000 dollars on his possession when detained. His story was a fact check by the officers taking selfies with him in his cell nicknaming him (Mr. 10 bands). To the right of me was a young lady arrested for fighting at a school G.E.D program with a security officer of the school. The third one was a meth user who had diabetes and who was homeless. You may be wondering why I mentioned these 3 people whose names I don't remember. Well thanks to them God use me to spread positive thoughts and ideas into their minds and focus not to give into bad and wicked temptations as there are real evils out in the world. God use them to keep me sane and hopeful. Reminding me no one is perfect and Thall shall not judge. That even when your made out to be a bad person let who you truly are shine.

Now I am not a psychology major, therapist or motivational speaker. I am young man who has face many adversities in life. Having no older siblings, no father growing up. Being bullied and having a religious family brings a lot of unsettling thoughts towards life. Rather than give into the bad in my life I have always used my own mistakes and sufferings to ensure that no one else I know or speak to feels the pain I have. Never been one too shy to speak to a stranger and say hey do you need some help. I bring this up because of the events that occur some people won't believe in unless they were there, and I can't blame them.

So, within fifteen minutes of me

being there, the young lady too, the right of me starts yelling, which I guess she has been doing until this point scheduled every 30 minutes. Cause the young man says here we go again and starts making jokes. They get into an argument and start throwing threats across the room. Fifteen more minutes now so I have been in here for about 45 minutes in a cell uncomfortable at this point I haven't sat in the cell bench. I haven't even had the chance to call my wife and let her know what has happened. Any who we get an officer switch at one pm eastern time which I did not know. So, the arresting officers never came to see me. New officers walk in and let us know we are going to be here until the morning when the van is out at court and not doing another drop-off till the morning. Get comfortable and stop the yelling ill bring you all some cigarettes and soda in a few minutes. Wait, I'm astounding pissed but I swallowed my pride. What else can I do at this moment. The two young lady and young man stop arguing and agree on some peace of mind when they agree to be quiet until the cigarettes get arrive.

Quiet and peaceful finally or so I thought. Now its questions time while we wait all I here. Hey sexy dread head what you in here for you mad quiet bro. I responded dumb found who me. The young lady and the young man responded yeah who else then they snicker and laugh. Off the back they both knew I was out of my element and was on it trying to see what they could get out of me. I told them straight up gun possession! The whole room went quiet bell tolls rang from the other side of the room all you hear is (damn homie you cooked) Spanish accent. I will mention this special person later. So now I break it down to them it's not what you think no gang banger or shooter just a husband and father who legally owns his gun. Being a person who was a victim of a failed home invasion. I have since made a practice to always keep my family safe. When we go on vacation and when they close their heads at night it's my duty to ensure they are safe. So as an American citizen I was using my right to bear arm with the actual and only purpose of protecting them from any situation that may occur in 2024 for. Now they understand who I am and are truly intrigued as to how they figured out I had a gun on me. Was it racism and the company thought I was stealing or did someone go behind your back and throw you under the bus. I was hoping it was neither because I did not inform no one of the mistake I made besides the text I sent to my wife explaining I am leaving early because I brought the wrong work items etc. I tell them what happened who knew. They agreed the worker who started with me snitched on me due to his color and being young just hating and still doesn't have the life experience to realize what he just done to an innocent man.

I then say enough about me as I don't want to think about why. As I will never wrap my mind as to why someone would intentionally destroy my life just to get ahead in a temporary situation. I can't believe a person whom I shared a meal with smoke with would really think of me as a lair or dangerous person. However, I was wrong the young man was racist and stereo type me used the information I shared with him about securing a gun in NJ as we both lived in the state. He has apologized about the whole situation, do I believe him no. That's another story. Got of subject but in a story every detail matters. Just like I explain here I also explained these feelings to the individuals detained I don't want to carry that type of anger with me. I feel it makes me weak as I can see him for who he is. Why would I allow him to break me a good kindhearted young man who always just trying to help. Versus him, a selfish individual who knows I have kids and a wife to support yet still made the decision to go through my things without my permission and state he was looking to use something of mine without asking me. Then snitch me out of the company thinking he would get rewarded.

So, they understand I'm hurt but all I can think about is my kids forget my life and how I am going to provide for them the way I have. I started crying in the cell thinking about all that comes with this my career down the drain nine years in the information technology gone who going to hire me. You would think I am about to get laughed at but know they all start to console me. Saying let it out its all-good big homie I believe you are one of those who will overcome this praying they drop your charges. Let me remind you we are now maybe four hours into me being there ten hours for the young lady and eight hours for the young man. The cigarettes arrive I take one to dry the tears and get rid of the smell of the cell and finally sit down. A few minutes later food arrives, if you can call it that. Frozen McDonalds that felt like eating rubber. Soda that the ice melted, and soda is now warm. I turned down the burger and stale fries and drink a sip of the beverage to keep me hydrated. Reality sets in I am in the system now, no rights no respect no humanity is what the treatment displayed by most workers. From this point, lawyers, lobby attendants, anyone not incarcerated now give this look of destain to all the people arrested without even knowing what or how it occurred. The law enforcement agents are even worse as they take enjoyment and pass the time by torturing the incarcerated. From bullying to taking pictures of them without consent to making it hard for those arrested to even contact their loved ones to let them know they have been detained.

I got off from the story again, the emotions that one feels when discussing this topic's situation are damn near impossible to tell you how much it hurts. Let's get back to the story though because it gets a little surreal. Like I still can't believe what I witness myself. Now with the food in hand emotions again are stirred by the other people being detained complaining over the food. Some say it's poisonous and that the police were trying to make them sick. Others just complain because they got one and not the other fries no burgers or burgers no fries. Most complaints still had let me out and where the officer is going to talk to me.

Bang sounds erupt as we hear the sound of someone being tossed around and fighting with the officers. In the cell one of the arrested people was able to sneak in his drugs and what he used to do the drugs. With the light of the cigarette, he was able to spark a flame and get high. Which he was caught amid using. They fought to recover the drugs and rest of substances from the user. He was already high enough one officer stated. They know label the man as suicide watch and remove him from the area. For our safety and his they state. Now we calm down just a little just to discuss what we all witness. For some it's normal to normal they know what's about to happen and don't even want to say. With me coming in while he was sleeping and throwing up. Those who were there before me seen more knew more of his behavior. Who am I to judge or say anything.

You would think that was it. Before the silence can enter the room. Ahhhh! screams from a female as if she is being beaten but no its not. She is screaming at the top of her lungs just to get the cops in the building because she and all of us are ignored regardless so now she pissed to the point where she doesn't care. She is just yelling to make everyone mad this happens for the next two hours the young lady take breaks every 30 mins or so then starts back. After two hours a cop comes in and tells her to be quiet or they are going to restrain her. She now in a belligerent state provoking the officer who are male. Making a statement like you just want to come here to feel me up when all I'm asking for a phone call. Calling them pig's perverts doing anything to entice a reaction from the officers. To the point I even get upset in my head (like shut the fuck up girl that's why you arrested now) I don't even know what she did but sheesh I no longer feel sorry. I understand her frustration but it's not going to do anything but get worst treatment for all of us.

Which one of the other detainees state out loud. Which she said she does not give a fuck what happens. Then doubles down on her behavior now get physical, hurting herself on the bars banging her head against the walls. She gets the officers attention now the male officers are currently on rotation and the female officers were out doing other things at that exact moment. This young lady knows the system which I soon find out. I thought the officers were going to get it under control. Was I wrong! within seconds of the officer requesting back up to restrain the young lady from causing herself any more bodily harm. She had stripped naked. Causing the officers to freeze in their tracks and request for female officers to come restrain her. Just like that the young lady got what she wanted. A female officer strong awesome black woman who is one of the first to not only humanize everyone. She spoke to the young lady with respect before asking her to do anything she ask her what's the problem. They talked compromised, which all she asks was to call someone in her family. The officer told her to get dress, and she will be back for her to make the call. She kept it honest and told us about the food situation and try to get fresher food.

The young lady was losing her mind because she needed to make arrangements for her kid, so nothing happened to the child while she was being detained and processed. Which she got into a fight with a security guard at Ged school she was attending. Which after she calms down and explains herself. The officer the lady gave her a hug, something she may not be allowed to do she did it anyway. The system hurts its people in so many ways it's hard for anyone to have hope. Finally, some peace and quiet and now at almost 9 pm at night I get to call my wife and let her know my situation. Let her know keep going to work, don't try to bail me out. I am going to give you all my account information and need you to withdraw everything I have.

Sell all my shit, you have my permission to do whatever you must to provide for our family I am so sorry I messed up like this. She couldn't process only concerned on the how it happened. I quickly let her know to snap it out. Hey I'm, good its okay I love you let me go and move on. She informs me she is not going anywhere. I let her know they are moving me to the courts house now I will get in touch with you soon as I can. I love you always will tell my boys I love them. Get some rest.

From one holding area to the next. New group new situations mixed with the young old from all over the 5 boroughs of NYC. Some cells holding over 20 people at a time. Let me tell you how blessed I was some sort of good power I call it my god, but we all have our own beliefs. The guards who escort us to the courts and are responsible for us till we are put into the next cell were amazing individuals. Being firm on the rules but being normal human beings understanding the difference between right and wrong, evil and good.

They talked to those who were willing to conversate. They allowed the leaders to look out for the elderly as we were chained to each other from hands down to the feet.

I learned about the changes within the systems like police officers being taken out of prisons and only correction officers in prisons and courts. I know made a (buddy) for those that don't know if you go to prison, you need a support system. To help you survive as best as you can in the situation. Not knowing what I was going into or how long I was going to be in there. I was already trying to build my mindset for the worst to come. God seeing that put a person that I wish to thank for being a big brother to me in that situation. When I went to sleep, he looked out and vice versa. We made sure we both got food, fruits and drinks when they were handed out.

Learned another important rule in the holding cells. Inmates are not allowed to touch each other even if you are attempting to save some one life. Which goes against everything I stand for. In the court holding cells you are face to face with everyone arrested and preparing to hear the charges they are facing and how to plead guilty or not guilty. When I say each process, itself is terrifying, causing numerous feelings to happen. Emotional roller coaster that lasts for what feels like forever until you leave the building free. You will face this emotional roller coaster of emotions such as. Anger frustrated you in the current predicament no matter how it occurred right or wrong on honest mistake.

Fear of what can happen to you while you're in there, what you are going to lose while you are in there, what everyone who is important to you is going to suffer. Shameful for what you've done, the way you are treated by the system, ashamed of the pain you caused to those around you and those involved in whatever situation you are facing. Depression as you don't know what's going to happen next and how much it's going to cost you to recover from the arrest process. Guilty or innocent it is costly once you have been charged with a crime, its more expensive to defend your innocence than it is to take a deal offered by the state.

So, while in the cell imagine you feeling any one of these things and you see fifteen to thirty people more feeling these same feelings. You can easily get overwhelmed with not knowing how to feel or what you see. So, on that note right in my cell right after they passed out lunch for the day. A young nicely dressed Asian man suit and tie fitted. Takes his suit jacket off places beneath his butt, sits down less than two minutes later starts to fall to ground having a seizure or stroke from a panic attack. I watched the whole thing before it occurred. Normally I would have reacted soon as I noticed and calmed him down to try to get them to breathe. Yet in this situation talking to him could make things worse.

    What felt like 30 seconds in my mind was 5 seconds. Where this young man cracks his head on the dirty jail floor and his tongue is sticking out of his mouth. He starts to bleed boom my mother and father teaching kick in. Being yelled at by the other cellmates don't touch him. I yell back I am not going to watch anyone die in front of me. I grabbed his suit jacket and rolled it up and put him on his side. Put the jacket over under his head to help prevent infection as his head was bleeding. Commanding that someone grab a guard's attention.

They get the guards' attention, and a group of guards come to help but first they make us get back for their safety. I get pulled out separately and the officer immediately knows I'm not used to this and scolds me at the same time commending me for saving the man's life even asking where I learned that from. Made a quick connection with him after telling him about my mother and father's professional background and he was intrigued to know more about me as a person. I share with him family heritage, nationality, and religious beliefs. What I do professionally and about our family's wife and kids etc.

This man and almost every other officer astounded that I am arrested. Shocked an all in disbelief that a young man like me even with the color tone of my skin would be consider a threat or a person who intentionally breaks the law. Honestly the people I spoke to are the only reason I got through this without committing suicide. Even if I was to have my cased dismissed the shame, I feel the things I seen experience just bought a hate to my life I am struggling every day to get rid of.

I am so thankful to the inmates, the officers and correction officers and the judge telling me I am a good person. Yet being a good person has no affect in the courts system. You may get leniency but that still won't change how your life will forever be impacted by a charge.

So much with the legal system is unjust and not formatted for each individual but to group a crime with a punishment. I don't disagree with crime and a punishment but there should also be other factors that take into account. Not just saying in my case but in all period. The court proceedings as it starts till it finishes is finically draining, time consuming and emotionally draining on everyone including those who are not part of the trial, the innocent bystanders. It's not efficient nor is it order. The trial process is like torture to everyone all the way to the judge.

I honestly don't think no one enjoys doing the job, maybe passionate but no way can you enjoy the wooden chairs, the stench in the building, the building heating and air system. Which if you see the equipment in half of these places you would have lots of questions. They are still running Windows 7 for most everything. So, it's performance is slow, hardware is outdated and constantly giving some sort of issues.

The staff is overworked, understaffed with not a minimum resources no real training given on applications or hardware. Paperwork is not properly kept causing constant time consumption by looking for items related to people. Most of the buildings bathrooms and water fountains never work. They are so overwhelmed they usually are always in a bad mood. Yet most of them are regular people not letting the power and authority go to their head. Which happens all over the world today. Let's talk about the trial. I think we spent enough time discussing the journey up until this point.

(Side note if anyone else facing situations like this lets come together and start and outreach community where we can share out stories pain with each other and help each other any way we can. This is my first opportunity and before I did this, I did my own research and seeing if there were any books like this there is not a lot. Definitely not like this one I write as the writer but will stop and be a reader just to share other thoughts that tie in with the message of the story, I am hoping to get across to the world.

    If you or anyone you know could use a resource like this, please share this with anyone willing to listen or read. If we don't come together cycles like this can never be broken. My heart goes out to all those underserved or wrongful accusations.)

Back to the Story!

[CHAPTER 3] THE TRIAL AND JOURNEY

The dates of the trial and the times will not be mentioned how many appearances and over the time span will be included. Such as I appeared in court a total of 15 times before the case was completed and the verdict and punishment had been given out to me. Once again, I will say this, I count my blessings because either way my situation could have been so much worst. What started out as a method of healing and dealing with the situation at hand I turned it into something to share with the world.

My survival story of a personal experience. So, I speak from a personal perspective of I believe in justice, but nothing is perfect. I don't want anyone to read this thinking I am against our system or the government, but a reform is needed in a sense we need human understanding and connections as a part of the process.

My first appearance in court was right before I was released from the holding cells, so I never made it to county jail or Rikers island. Some people may not know this but the courts in most states can hold detainee up to the thousands and you can be there for days at a time. Close to a week can be in the holding cells of a court and another week in the police station holding cell. You would not believe how many holding cells there are in the United States alone. Crime pays just not the criminals who are doing the time.

 Off track once again. My first appearance is being told what I am charged with and when I can appear to put my verdict guilty not guilty in. 3 months away from that day. So, for 3 months I'm like before the system sees my info let me find a job. Which I did God came through for me in ways I have to explain.

 I got a job inside the train station at the world trade center. Paying good and treated good so I end up getting my first welcome gift grom a company. I was sent flowers to my home and a welcome letter of encouragement. Tiffany she such a great and sweet person for legal purposes.

I will not mention the name of the company I worked for during this time. I am grateful for the opportunity they gave me and the time I worked for them. Which I was able to end the trial while working for them. Once I was convicted, they decided to part ways and paid me for a few months to stay afloat, which they didn't have to. So outside of actual court proceedings I had to pick up paperwork pick up date for court orders and then pay fines and sign release forms etc. such as bonds.

I had no bond, just what I call a pre probation system newly added. Where they help you look for jobs and give you mental health support etc. Which was like a halfway house in my opinion. That process was five visits itself before all was said and done. Which greatly appreciated how much they supplied fare for public transportation. There are a lot of pros and cons about the system.

Meaning I wouldn't see it removed in fact I commend the fireman, policeman and medical workers

EMT's first responders out here are doing things on the right side of humanity with consideration for others while still protecting their wellbeing and civilians and other around not just in the moment but at all times. The officers helping build communities not destroy a group of people for any hidden agenda. I thank you all because it's the human people who give us hope in these darkest of moments.

Each process or time spent in court is interstate traveling from NJ – NY about one hour and 30 mins each way minimum. Four hours minimum at court expect to be there for eight hours some time longer. You can be in court from the time it opens to the time it closes and would wish that no one. What's worst you can wait a whole day for nothing and have to come back the next business day to do it all over again even if it's the day and time you were scheduled for. So, you lose a day of work or two each time you go.

I can say this in the courts though its draining if you look from the outside and think about other people situations before yours you start to understand the system. Such as the number of cases a judge has seen vs the amount of times a person thinks this has never happened. To the amount of violent out breaks that occur from the defendant to the plaintiff to the stuff in between. I understand it, I sympathize with it. I am writing to advocate for anyone who needs help just to hold on. I'll explain why it's how I survived what gave me hope to write this and keep moving forward towards the goals I set out towards.

The trial process was not as bad as the arrest and the cell incarceration moments. I was free and able to move around still live. I had my wife who was not leaving my side no matter what is to come. My family, in spite of circumstances didn't judge or make me feel less of a person instead encourage me to let who I am as a person shine that will overcome anything. This dark cloud that was lurking felt like my options were limited in my life. With all that being said the trial was a make it break it moment. Questioning daily am I even worth it. Like my kids would be better if I was dead at this moment. Every time I had to go into the building that was the feeling left.

How would you deal with a situation like this, and you haven't even faced the charges yet. I learn to look for the little moments no matter where you at when you don't belong even if you can't see it everyone else around you can. They will let you know one way or another I learn to look for the positive you don't belong, being respected for who I am more than anything is all I have. So having manners, always keeping a smile, and being polite, while still keeping ties to my roots and community. I was able to build a spiritual shield that allows me to walk into corporate buildings as myself and be treated like the owner of the company. I take pride in that power and expand on it. So, when I sat down in the court with my wife, my son I showed who I was loving dad, respecting husband, and the courteous stranger. Which I may not gotten charges drop but on record the judge commended me as a person a man. She apologized for what happened and that the system is imperfect. She gave me the best conditions in the worst situations. My public defender even apologized for the horrible job he did. He knew as a black man he looked at me as just a job. Which I know that was still just the job talking but he could just say good luck. Every officer I dealt with eventually spoke to me a few gave me a few personal numbers which I hope I never have to use.

A year has passed since the arrest and a few months about 14 months for the full trial to end and me to get my sentencing. Which was as follow Probation for 3 years minimal visits no restrictions for flights or work. My car license was not suspended, she gave me the information to have my case removed from my record and put me into another new program that would ensure I won't be a felon for the rest of my life.

So yeah, guys, I pleaded guilty to owning my own legal gun that I accidentally forgot to ensure it was safely secure which I was truly guilty of. Will I let this stop me? Heck no! I will rise above this and keep my word to my family. How will I make it out find out in the next book the "The Probation" thanks for reading.

THE END

Never give up on yourself

anything is possible.

"Believe it"

S. AUSTIN JR - THE GUN CHARGE -44

Samuel Austin

Stage Name: U_no\ DJ Black Mask

Brooklyn NY Native

Owner of Kid2adults non-profit

Dancer/ Rapper /Martial artist/ Music producer

Co-founder of Brokuza anime community group. Full time Dad, Fulltime husband, Fulltime computer technician, part time song writer, part time poet. Part time DJ amateur still. Always here for my family and friends can't tell you I wouldn't be half the man I am today without you all.

Thank you and shoutouts.

First and foremost, Jehovah I thank you for watching over me all my life.

1. My mother Michelle, far from perfect, never gave up

2. My father's Sam and John thank you both for showing me the rights and wrongs.

3. To my sons Josiah and Ezran, I thank you for being you and loving me as dad in a way only you guys can.

4. My wife Qua'desha words will never express how grateful and how much I appreciate you. I'm so honored to spend

each day with you and so looking forward to what the future has installed for us.

5. To my friend Rodderick you started this bond of friendship that encourages one another we have been trying to live up to the image and energy you brought into this world May you rejoice in heaven up above

   I know you got God cracking up right now.

6. To my brother from another Mother Felix, I love you for being a brother when I needed it. A friend, and wing man, a

mentor, and most of all for still being a friend when I didn't deserve it.

7. To my brother Saban and little sister Elaina thanks for being the best sibling an older brother can ask for never had to worry about either one.

8. To my cousins all over the world Trey, lil Tee, Charny, Alex, Domonique, Stacy, Deandra and Denise, the little ones. Jada Bada my cousins in Belize Taysha and Tevin I love you all and so proud to be related to you all some I didn't mention but you're in my thoughts and thanks to.

9. To my aunts, uncles and extended family I love you all and thank you all for the love and support over the years. Last but not least My grandmothers and one grandfather will not mention y'all names lol cause y'all all grumps to the 3 grandmothers in

my life I love you all so much. The lessons you each have imparted in me will be lessons I forever pass on to the next generation.

Go way just a random poem I wrote during the first days of the situation wanting the tears to go away. Life throws you a lot of unseen circumstances, my thoughts your never as alone as you think.

Go Away

Go Away Go Away

If only this could be thrown away.

Once it comes to light it can be cast as shade.

Got damn it! Stube my toe at the grocery store.

Hold it lord take it lord don't let it break shit.

Kids working on my nerve.

Wife giving me chores galore.

God these blessings I pray to stay.

Racism, hating and they even know him!

Fake friends move like Satan go behind your back call it taken.

Betrayed then played yet "Uncle
Ruckus" No relation!
What I'm saying is the real and there
the fakest.
The pain that we take in and the pain
we can take in.
Pain go way save we really need
another way!

A poem dedicated to Qua'desha, the love of my life, my soul mate, the person who sets my soul on fire and is the fuel that keeps me going. This is all possible because of her.

For you

I won't stop no matter what.
To rise and be true a force I never

knew.

A person I didn't see came into

existence.

Took pieces of different puzzles and

made a work of art.

No luck this is spiritual only gods

excellence.

I mean a brute to Mr. Tech. From Mr. Hated too nothing but love and respect.

Won't even speak on the sex.

Yes, its blessed blessed blessed. No more stress just liven loving each moment with you cause of you and for you!

A poem I wrote when I was 14- 15 inspired by the death of my aunt and her son who was incarcerated during the funeral of his mother. This still resonates to me this day. As it's a moment in time I can never unshaken seeing a man till this day I respect and look at as one of the strongest men out here both physically and mentally. Seeing him break down while in hand cuffs at the sight of his mom in a casket. The humbleness in him when asking the correction officers to uncuff one hand so he can hug his mother one last time. Never gave it a title. It's been published before. So, I will change it to fit who I am now.

No Lie

Tell me the truth and I will tell you no lie.
Gangsters don't go to heaven and thugs don't cry.

God why am I living here just to die.

So much pain and disease

Yet I choose to stand then to leave.

Please lord help me help us save my family.

Give my friend peace and everything we need.

Keep the ones who are gone as close as can be.

God use me in any way you see need to achieve.

A world we can live in and only live.

Till I see all my loved ones lost again.

There is no End!

List of songs I love to listen to any time any mood got me through music

1. Artist: Gpytian Song: "serious Times"

2. Artist: Labrinth Song: "Mount Everest"

3. Artist: Benson Boone Song:" Beautiful

Things"

4. Artist: Khantrast Song: 'Kazekage"

5. Artist: Tems Song: "Free Mind"

6. Artist: Big Sean ft lil Wayne Song "Deep"

7. Artist: Teddy Swims Song: "Lose Control"

8. Artist: Steve Lacey Song: "Bad habit"

9. Artist: Fridayy Song: "Stand By Me"

10. Artist: Fridayy Song: "Mercy"

11. Artist: Fridayy and Chris brown Song: "Don't Give it Away"

The Gun Charge. PREDICATION

To start with this is not a fairy tale. No Run them up gang banger story. Just a mistake turned into tragedy. Ordinarily you hear these stories word of mouth from a friend, a family member or in passing. I come to you from my personal story of pain and suffering. The reflection and refusal to lose. My overcoming throughout the trial as it began and concluded. Even the before what led to things that never make it to trial. I am writing this because I did not have an outlook, no one to turn to for advice on the situation do not get me wrong. I have a lot of support emotionally, mentally, and spiritually. Yet I was missing an understanding of what I experienced, going through. The moments that have impacted on my family, my would my character. Rather than losing myself, I choose to write my feelings to you.

We start with the main character of the story, Uno, father of two. Married to lady wild card. They share one kid together and uno has another kid with the queen of spades. The queen of spades and uno share and 12-year-old name Dos. Which is a story for another day. Lady wild card and uno have a 4-year-old name Uno jr. At this time in his life Uno is a well-respected diligent father. Who has earned some rewards in life! The story takes place in the present. Also, how we got to this point presently. Will open my beliefs on certain situations having to face them firsthand. From attempted home invasion to being robbed at gun point. Things a lot of people suffer trauma scars for life. From environmental life to unfortunate circumstances while vacationing.

I am taking my story and telling you why I can stay positive no matter what tribulations I face. Inspired by my friends to write and tell my story Rest in peace Eric Breezy Baker. In loving memory, I kept our word and published one of the works we spoke on.

Made in the USA
Columbia, SC
29 April 2025